THE
FIELD&
STREAM
Fly Fishing
Handbook

The *Field & Stream* Fishing and Hunting Library

FISHING

The Field & Stream *Baits and Rigs Handbook* by C. Boyd Pfeiffer

The Field & Stream *Bass Fishing Handbook* by Mark Sosin and Bill Dance

The Field & Stream *Fish Finding Handbook* by Leonard M. Wright Jr.

The Field & Stream *Fishing Knots Handbook* by Peter Owen

The Field & Stream *Fly Fishing Handbook* by Leonard M. Wright Jr.

The Field & Stream *Tackle Care and Repair Handbook* by C. Boyd Pfeiffer

FORTHCOMING TITLES

HUNTING

The Field & Stream *Bow Hunting Handbook* by Bob Robb

The Field & Stream *Deer Hunting Handbook* by Jerome B. Robinson

The Field & Stream *Firearms Safety Handbook* by Doug Painter

The Field & Stream *Shooting Sports Handbook* by Thomas McIntyre

The Field & Stream *Turkey Hunting Handbook* by Philip Bourjaily

The Field & Stream *Upland Bird Hunting Handbook* by Bill Tarrant

Books by Leonard M. Wright Jr.

Fishing the Dry Fly as a Living Insect

Fly-Fishing Heresies

Where the Fish Are

The Ways of Trout

First Cast

Superior Flies

Stonefly and Caddis Fly Fishing

The Masters on the Nymph (co-editor)

Neversink

The Field & Stream *Treasury of Trout Fishing* (editor)

The Fly Fisher's Reader (editor)

The Field & Stream *Fish Finding Handbook*

The Field & Stream *Fly Fishing Handbook*

THE
FIELD & STREAM
Fly Fishing
Handbook

Leonard M. Wright Jr.

Illustrated by Richard Harrington

THE LYONS PRESS

Originally published as *First Cast: The Beginner's Guide to Fly Fishing* in 1987 by Fireside, a division of Simon & Schuster, Inc., by arrangement with Nick Lyons Books.

First Lyons Press edition—1999

Printed in the United States of America

10 9 8 7 6 5 4 3 2 1

Library of Congress Cataloging-in-Publication Data

Wright, Leonard M.
    [First cast]
    The Field & stream fly-fishing handbook / Leonard M. Wright Jr. ;
illustrated by Richard Harrington.
        p.   cm.—(Field & stream fishing and hunting library)
    Originally published: First cast. New York : Simon & Schuster,
c1987.
    Includes bibliographical references (p. 103) and index.
    ISBN 1-55821-897-1
    1. Fly fishing.   I. Field & stream.   II. Title.   III. Title:
Field and stream fly-fishing handbook.   IV. Title: Fly-fishing
handbook.   V. Series.
SH456.W69   1999
799.1'24—dc21   98-45446
                                                          CIP

Contents

"It is the constant—or inconstant—change, the infinite variety in fly fishing that binds us fast. It is impossible to grow weary of a sport that is never the same on any two days of the year."

—THEODORE GORDON (1914)

Preface

IT HAS ALWAYS struck me as cruelly unfair that the reader always knows precisely who he is and how much knowledge he has, while the long-suffering author never has a clue about who is going to pick up his book. I'm going to level the playing field, this time, by presuming to know who you are and what you're up to.

First, I'll assume that you're not an expert fly fisher, but would fall into either the "beginner" or "intermediate" category. This will allow me to omit a lot of hairsplitting, technical points that are nearly impossible to describe in print, anyway. I'll stick to the most important things you should know, do, and *not* do to become a "very good" angler.

Second, I'm taking it for granted that you're right-handed, simply because I happen to be. Therefore, in any instructions, I will refer to the right arm as the casting arm and to the left hand as the line hand. If you happen to be a southpaw, I apologize, but I'm sure that, by now, you're well adjusted to such high-handedness from the right.

Third, you may feel that I put too much emphasis on flowing, fresh water—brooks, streams, and rivers. But I'm doing that on purpose, because three-quarters of all fly fishing is practiced on running water. Lake, pond, and saltwater situations won't be ignored. However, I'll have to tailor the coverage to the type of fishing you're most likely to be doing.

Finally, this is not meant to be either armchair reading or an encyclopedia. There are already thousands of books giving vivid experiences and exhaustive details on every aspect of the sport. Some of the most useful of these are listed in appendix 7. Rather, this is intended as a "first word." Tuck it in your pocket or vest and take it along when you go fishing. It's a small book, no bigger or heavier than the average fly box. I hope what's inside will catch you more fish than the contents of any fly box you ever carry.

1

Why Fly?

"How do I love thee? Let me count the ways."
—Elizabeth Barrett Browning

IN THE BEGINNING was the fly rod—or at least its primitive ancestor. We have graphic proof that "fishing poles" are 5,000 years old, or nearly as ancient as the fishhook itself. Early rods swung the hook out to where the fish were and hauled the captives back, and that is essentially all today's high-tech graphite rods are accomplishing.

Other forms of casting are surprisingly modern and totally different. All cast a relatively heavy weight and here, the lighter the line, the longer the cast. The bait-casting, or revolving-spool, reel is some 200 years old and the fixed-spool, spinning reel is only about 100. For centuries, fishing with a rod meant fishing with a fly rod of some sort.

Artificial flies aren't quite so ancient. We have written proof that they were in use nearly 2,000 years ago and they may be much older than that. Very early in the fishing game, anglers noticed that stream and river fish were extremely fond of the aquatic insects that lived in, and hatched out on, the water. They also discovered that these small, fragile mayflies, caddisflies, and stoneflies turned into a gooey mess when they tried to impale them on a hook.

Some long-forgotten genius concocted a fake fly by winding more durable feathers onto his hook and then played this in or on the water to act like the real thing. It worked—or worked often enough—and fly fishing was born.

It was soon discovered that a long, limber rod helped to switch

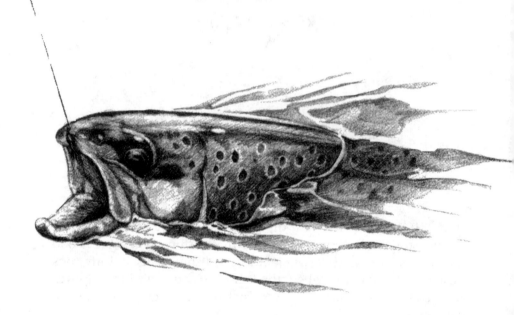

this fly farther out over the water. And experiments showed that a relatively fat, heavy line (except for a short, thin portion next to the fly) was needed to relay the energy of the rod, and that the nearly weightless artificial fly would then go along for the ride.

Fly fishing imposes several restrictions on the angler and yet, paradoxically, it is these limitations that make it so much more fun. The fly rod is a short-range weapon. Its maximum range is only a fraction of the surf-casting rod's. It is also basically a shallow-water method. Admittedly, we now have fast-sinking and lead-core fly lines that permit some dredging, yet more than 95 percent of all fly fishing is done with floating lines that limit lure travel to the top layers of water.

A lure that is both near the angler and near the surface dictates a highly visual game. Frequently, you're casting to a fish, or its swirl, that you have observed. Often you can see the fish take your fly, as well. Seeing is half the fun in fishing. That's why comparatively few people enjoy night fishing. Fishing with a floating fly is widely considered the cream of the game. Not because it's in any way more sporting. It's just more visual. One take on the surface is worth two you merely feel.

Since you're casting at close range to seen or suspected fish, the sheer luck of chuck-and-chance-it is also greatly reduced. Stealth, dexterity, and, some might add, intellect are rewarded. Fly rodding is a thinking man's fishing.

Short and shallow doesn't mean you'll be shortchanged in results, though. In many situations, fly fishing is the deadliest method. A river I frequently fish flows into a large reservoir, and where the current flow starts to slow down marks a well-known and heavily fished hot spot for large, lake-dwelling trout. Nearly every time I fish there, I enjoy the company of several spin fishermen who are whizzing out the most popular lures. Yet I always (except when everyone goes

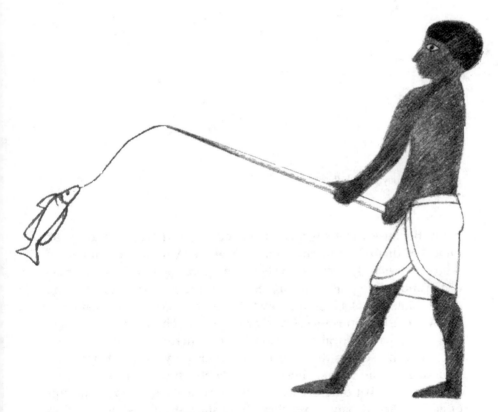

Early "fly fisherman"—from an Egyptian wall painting.

A 16th-century English fly.

blank because the fish haven't moved up in there) outcatch the bunch of them. Not because I'm a magician. A frequent companion who's a novice fly caster outfishes them, too. Apparently the translucence and subtle pulsations of a good streamer fly make it a far more deadly imitation of a bait minnow than any wood or metal creation.

While fishing in France, I was fortunate enough to get to know, and fish with, a pair of local, professional trout fishermen. They made their livelihood by selling the wild brown trout they caught from hard-pounded, public rivers. These anglers were frighteningly effective. French law, at that time, allowed them to use any bait or method short of gill nets and dynamite, yet they chose smallish, insect-imitating flies 95 percent of the time to earn their daily baguette.

Fishing with flies can become an education in itself. The deeper you get into it, the more you'll want to learn. Your first step is likely to be collecting and studying the aquatic insects that fish feed on. The next thing you know, you're into fly tying, then on to poultry raising, which can lead you into genetics to improve the stiffness and color of hackle feathers. Curiosity about stream fertility and habitat improvement pull you quickly into biology, water chemistry, geology, hydrology, and forestry. The domino effects in fly fishing can lead you down all sorts of primrose paths—and surprisingly enriching ones.

Not long ago, fly fishing was considered elitist. Live-bait fishermen thought fly fishers were snobs and, unfortunately, they were right in many cases. In late-19th-century England, fly fishing, especially dry-fly fishing, turned into an ethical, even moral, issue. This pecksniffian purism quickly flowed across the Atlantic, polluting our shores—or at least the eastern one—for decades.

Two factors started to change all this shortly after World War II. Newly developed synthetics—fiberglass for rods, plastic coatings for lines, and monofilament for leaders—replaced the organic materials: bamboo, silk, and gut. The new outfits were cheaper, tougher, and virtually maintenance-free. This helped enormously to bring fly fishing off its artificial pedestal and down to earth.

Then, too, there were now more people fishing for far fewer fish. Many decided to fish for fun rather than for food. This new philosophy brought many new recruits to fly casting, because it is the only fishing method that is a joy whether you catch fish or (God forbid!) not. Try dunking a worm from an anchored rowboat all day long and you'll see what I mean.

I could go on and on, but any list of fly fishing's rewards and virtues pales before the late Arnold Gingrich's crisp pronouncement: "Fly fishing is the most fun you can have standing up."

Setting Out and Setting Up

*"Ther ben twelve manere of ympedymentes
whyche cause a man to take noo fysshe . . .
the fyrst is yf your harnays be not mete
nor fetly made."*

—Dame Juliana Berners

MOST FINANCIAL columnists I read complain that we Americans are compulsive consumers. We save less and run up more personal debt than the citizens of any other industrialized nation in the world, they say.

I'm now going to do my part in trying to reverse that trend. If you're about to take up fly fishing, do not—repeat, do not—rush to your nearest tackle store and pig out. Resist the temptation until you've acquired more knowledge and some sort of casting style of your own.

Instead, try to borrow a decent outfit from a friend who's an experienced fly caster. Don't be afraid to ask. After all, you're not begging for the loan of his wife or toothbrush. Just a reasonable fly fishing outfit. The chances are he already possesses more of these than he'll admit to around the house, including some he hasn't used in years.

If he seems reluctant, go straight to gambit II. Suggest that he take you fishing so that he can personally supervise and safeguard his property. This is where you should end up anyway—free equipment plus free lessons. Only the most flint hearted of fisherpersons can resist such wheedling and cajoling. Fly fishers are born proselytizers,

resist such wheedling and cajoling. Fly fishers are born proselytizers, all too willing to spread the faith.

RODS

The best or easiest rod to learn with is one that's relatively long and has a slow and forgiving action. I couldn't recommend one under 8 feet, and one of 9 or more might be better if you have a choice. All things being equal, a longer rod bends more, making it easier for you to feel how it's working during the cast. A flabby rod is a disaster, but one with a "slow" action—meaning that it bends throughout most of its length instead of mainly in the tip section—will help you feel the cast better, too.

LINES

The fly line must be matched carefully to the action of the rod. This is so important that rods are usually described by the line weight they take as well as their length. The line scale runs from the lightest, 1, up through the heaviest, 15. The code refers to the weight of the front 30 feet of that particular line. The lightest you're likely to encounter fall into the 3- to 4-weight class. Many prefer these for casting tiny flies on glassy limestone or spring creeks. Most rough-stream anglers choose slightly stouter outfits in the 5- to 6-weight range. Those who cast bulky streamer flies and bass bugs on still waters seem to prefer 7- or 8-weights. Saltwater fly casters usually choose rods that handle 8- to 10-weight lines and some, like those who cast for giant tarpon, swear by 12-weights.

All good fly lines are tapered. The double taper starts out relatively fine, increases diameter gradually for 6 to 10 feet, then runs fat and level for most of its length before dropping down into a short taper again. This type of line is ideal for gently placing small flies on tranquil water, to spooky fish. If one end of a double-taper line gets cracked or worn, you can reverse it on the reel and fish with an identical, unused section.

Weight-forward, bug, or saltwater tapers are one-ended, though. They taper more quickly up to a fat, belly portion that, after about 25 feet, tapers down into a thin running line for the rest of their length,

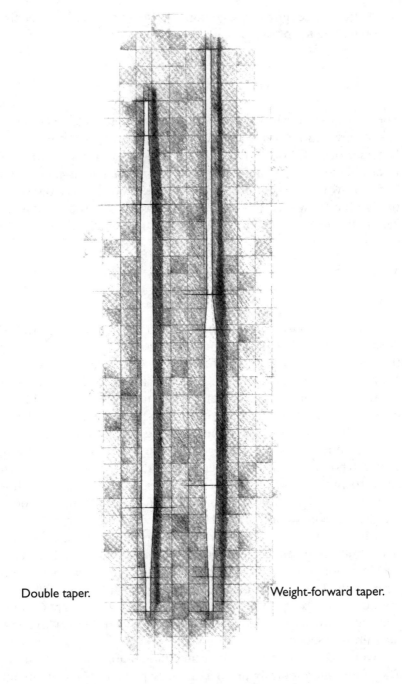

Double taper.

Weight-forward taper.

Both lines are greatly fattened to emphasize their differences.

which shoots more easily through the rod guides. Despite some disadvantages, this type of taper helps you get casting line out quicker, gives you slightly more distance, and makes casting bulky lures easier. The illustration compares these two basic line types.

REELS

Most fly reels are relatively simple affairs: They serve mainly to store the line you're not casting or holding in your left hand. A single-action model (one turn of the handle equals one turn of the spool) with a minimum drag will suffice for nearly all freshwater fishing. For salmon, steelhead, and large saltwater species, you may need a reel with a strong, adjustable drag, though in some cases a multiplier (a reel in which one complete turn of the handle results in more than one turn of the spool) can come in handy.

LEADERS

Your leader should continue the taper in the front end of your fly line down to a thin section nearest the fly. You can buy ready-made leaders at most tackle stores. They come in many diameters and several lengths—9 feet being the most common. Some taper down to as fine as 1-pound test while stouter ones, for saltwater use, may end up at 12-pound test or even stronger. The size of the fly you're going to cast and the fish you expect to catch will dictate the size you put on that day. You'll also need some spools of monofilament in several weight categories to vary the thickness of your tippet (the very end of the leader) or to renew it.

KNOTS

There are dozens of fishing knots, but for fly fishing only three knots are essential. The Improved Turle is best for up- and down-eyed hooks, while the improved clinch is superior for straight-eyed models. For tying two pieces of monofilament together, use the blood knot. All three knots are fairly easy to tie with a bit of practice; the diagrams will show you how.

Turle knot. The forward loop is pulled tight into a knot, then the rear loop is passed over the fly and tightened around the neck of the hook.

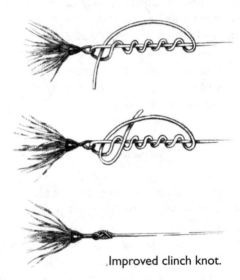

Improved clinch knot.

Blood (or barrel) knot.

FLIES

We have now, finally, reached the business end of your tackle. The fly, after all, is the only part of your inventory that any fish should ever see. Flies come in all sizes, shapes, and colors, but they can be grouped into five basic styles that are easy to recognize.

Dry flies are tied on light-wire hooks; they have upright wings and a bushy collar of stiff hackle (rooster neck feather) to help them float on the surface. Wet flies are usually tied on heavier hooks with wings and sparse, soft hackle sloping back toward the bend of the hook, and are designed to sink quickly under the surface. So are nymphs, which are imitations of the larval stages of aquatic insects. These look much like wet flies without wings. Streamers (and bucktails) are large, long, and slim and represent various types of minnows. Last, bass bugs (and poppers) are big, bulky, and made out of deer hair, cork, balsa wood, hollow plastic, or various combinations of these so that they will float on the surface. Some recommended patterns and sizes of all five types are listed in appendix 2.

WADERS AND ACCESSORIES

Equipment for fly fishing rarely ends with just the basic tackle, however. Since you're going to be on, or in, the water, you'll need help in keeping dry.

In some cases, this calls for a boat. A canoe may be your best choice for small lakes or ponds. At the top end of the scale are bluewater sportfishing boats that can cost up to a million dollars fully equipped. It all depends on where you fish, how elegant you wish to be, and what you can afford.

More often, you'll need only hip boots or chest waders to separate you from the chilly water. Boots are fine for brooks and small streams. Larger streams, rivers, lake margins, and surf usually call for waders. Whichever you end up with, get ones with felt on their bottoms where they come in contact with slippery rocks. They can spare you uncomfortable, sometimes dangerous, dunkings when you're negotiating slimy rocks. There are a few notoriously treacherous streams where metal cleats or chains are a virtual necessity. There are also some with sandy or gravelly bottoms where regular rubber bottoms are satisfactory, but for all-around work, I'd put my

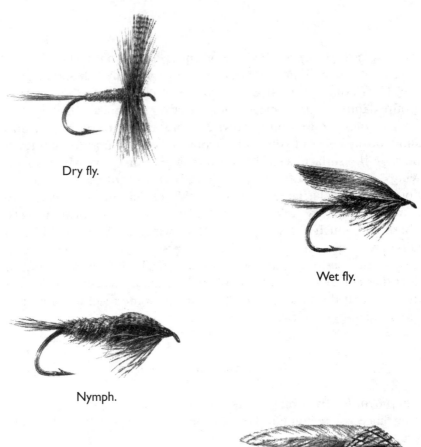

Dry fly.

Wet fly.

Nymph.

Streamer fly.

Popping bass bug, with heavy piece of monofilament positioned as a weedguard.

rubber bottoms are satisfactory, but for all-around work, I'd put my money on felts.

You should have a pair of glasses for eye protection, and polarized sunglasses, which cut the glare and let you see beneath the surface, are usually the best choice.

Fly fishers seem to have a special weakness for accessories and gadgets. (Perhaps those hand-wringing economists are right, after all.) You'll find a list of necessities and sometimes-useful extras in appendix 4. You decide how much you want to lug around.

RIGGING

Before you actually start fishing, you have to rig up your tackle and, even here, there are Dos and Don'ts. There are several ways to knot or splice your leader to your fly line and this to the backing line that fills up your reel spool. All will slip through your rod guides easily, but there's a better way to make these connections.

Since nearly all leaders come with loops on their heavy ends, you can change them much more easily if there's a loop in the end of your fly line, too. Simply insert one loop through the other and pull the rest of the leader on through and you have a firm, neat attachment. The same system works for your line-to-backing linkage. The illustration on the next page shows you how to whip on these loops. I'd recommend a loop of 20-pound-test monofilament for the leader end of your fly line. A small length of backing—that lighter, limper bait-casting line you use to fill up the reel spool underneath your fly line—makes a neater connection on the other end. Just double the backing line back on itself and fasten it into a loop by the same method. Make sure this is large enough—6 to 8 inches should do—to pass over the reel.

When stringing the line through the guides, double back the first few inches of fly line and poke this highly visible part through each guide in turn. You're much more likely to skip a guide if you try doing this with the nearly invisible monofilament leader. And before you knot on your chosen fly, make a final inspection to make sure you haven't missed a guide or spiraled the line around the rod someplace. It is surprisingly easy to foul up this simple process if you're trying to rig up when fish are rising all around you!

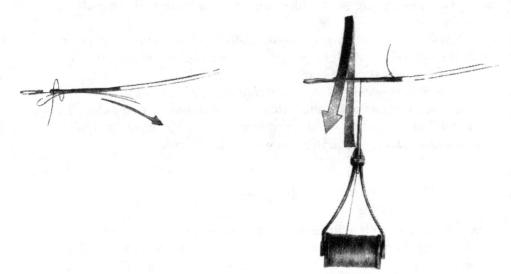

Wind several wraps of thread back over thread end, then trim end. Wind several turns over thread loop, insert thread end through loop, then pull loop and thread through windings. Clip flush and varnish well.

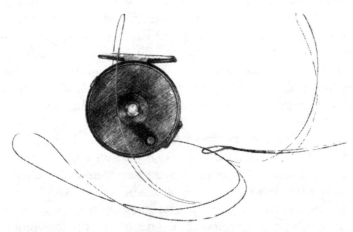

Insert backing loop through smaller line loop, pass backing loop over reel, then pull tight.

A rigged-up rod, ready for along-stream travel.

Now hook your fly in the first, or stripping, guide of your rod, run the leader around the rim of the reel, and then reel in the slack until the line is tight. Don't put the fly in that small keeper ring many rod makers place just in front of the grip. It's far more likely to hook one of your fingers there, and it will also mash the hackles of a good dry fly.

Now that you're finally rigged up and headed for the river, here's a last tip. Carry your rod pointed forward: It's by far the easiest way during daylight hours. Tip pointed rearward may be safer for the rod when you're feeling your way back to your car after dark, but be fore-warned, you'll hang up on far more twigs and branches that way. When you must carry the rod butt-first, make sure the line is still rigged through the guides and the hook is firmly attached. Otherwise, when your rod gets hung up in the bushes, the tip section may get pulled loose. Then it's lost and gone forever.

CHAPTER

Casting

*"The faults one naturally looks for in
a learner are taking the rod too far back
and not waiting until the instant when the line
is extended."*

—Eric Taverner

CASTING WITH A fly rod, when done properly and automatically, is one of the great joys of fly fishing. Its motion is fluid, graceful, gratifying, and, like virtue, is a reward to itself. However, it takes a lot of concentration and practice to become an expert caster, and it's not really easy to become even a good one.

For the complete novice, learning to cast well takes determination. Despite the fact that there are entire books devoted to this art and that most start out with the assumption that the reader has never cast a line before, I frankly don't believe that fly casting can be taught from scratch by printed words and pictures. Get an experienced friend or a fishing school to help you through the early stages. This will spare you hours of agony and frustration.

If this is, indeed, to be your very first try, string up the fly rod, attach a leader of about 9 feet, tie on a fly (preferably one with the point and bend snapped off), and pull 20 feet or so of line out beyond the rod tip. Now have your instructor/friend make several casts and explain carefully what he's doing. This will give you some inkling of what you're going to try to duplicate.

After a few of the basics have sunk in, take the rod in your own hand and grip it properly, thumb up, as pictured on page 21. Grasp it

other residents when it charges up the pool. Always look, plan, and scheme before you step into a stream.

Fish in larger rivers are usually less spooky, but it still pays to stalk them with respect. They can't hear your above-water voice, no matter how loudly you shout, but they can hear a pin drop under water. Don't scuff your feet, and stay off teetering rocks that could send a warning noise ahead of you.

Fish have a blind spot directly to their rear. Since stream-dwelling fish always head into the current, this allows you to get quite close to fish upstream of you. Crinkled water obscures a fish's above-water vision and lets you get even closer. However, when you're fishing a sunken fly across and downstream toward fish facing in your direction, it's wise to cast a fairly long line.

A slow, quiet pool calls for extra caution. Glide into position slowly and gracefully. If you send out rings of telltale ripples, fish will be alerted. They may not dive under a rock or race upstream, but they probably won't look at a fly, either, for 15 to 20 minutes after becoming suspicious.

It's always wise to stay as low as possible, even if you have to crouch. Never allow yourself to be silhouetted against the skyline. There's little advantage in wearing camouflage, but do avoid light-colored or bright clothing. A white hat is the worst thing you can put on your head. Avoid any unnecessary motions—especially abrupt ones—and try to advance directly toward a fish. This will make your approaching form appear nearly motionless. And don't be too proud to kneel while casting.

You may think the act of wading is as simple as merely walking through water, but it's not. Most underwater stones are slippery, and big, flat ones are notoriously so. Avoid them wherever possible. Try to plant your feet on the fine gravel that collects between larger rocks. And resist the temptation to wade out deeper by using the tops of underwater boulders as stepping-stones. That's risky business. If you must try it, be sure you have a change of clothing nearby.

Strong currents can make wading difficult, but there are ways to reduce their force. Stand sideways to the flow. Your legs and body offer less water resistance in this position. (That's also a good point for ocean waders to remember when they see an especially large wave bearing down on them.) Move one foot at a time; only when that one is securely planted should you move the other one. Move the upstream foot first, then bring the other up next to, but never ahead of, it. A wading staff, or one improvised from a stout stick, can be a big help in high, fast water. The best wading advice of all, though, is "When in doubt—don't."

BOAT FISHING

Most lake and saltwater anglers usually operate out of some sort of boat, and I'll have to assume you're proficient at handling your chosen craft. It's not within the scope of this book to teach you how to paddle your canoe or dock your 48-foot Hatteras.

There are, however, several specialized Dos and Don'ts that the boater-turned-fisher should keep in mind. First of all, make a point of being quiet. Ship your oars or put down your paddle noiselessly when you're approaching fish. Lower your anchor softly, too. Any splash or thump will put nearby fish on the qui vive. I once spooked a school of bonefish that were more than 100 feet away by clumsily dropping my Zippo onto the bottom of a flats boat.

If you're using a motor, turn it off well before you reach the intended fishing area, then coast or scull your way in. A few species of fish may seem undisturbed by engine or propeller noises, but most of them know better.

In choppy water, waves slapping against the side of your boat can alert nearby fish. You can sometimes cut down this annoyance by pointing your boat bow-first into the waves. And, of course, in a flat calm avoid sending out advance-warning ripples.

In the shallows or on the flats, the boat angler has an advantage over the wader. He has a higher viewing point and can pick out fish at a greater distance. On the other hand, fish can spot him from farther away, too. Even here, it sometimes pays to cast from a crouch or a kneeling position. And don't try to get as close to a fish as you might when you're wading.

CHAPTER 6

Presentation

"Be still, moving your flies upon the water."
—Izaak Walton

EVEN THOUGH you have dropped your fly onto the water at precisely the right time and place, you still have to convince the fish that your offering is, indeed, lean red meat and not just a fraudulent bunch of fur and feathers. Exactly what you now do or, rather, make your fly do will depend on what sort of food you're trying to imitate and what species of fish you're trying to fool.

DRY FLY ON RUNNING WATER

The dry, or floating, fly is one of the most effective lures for stream fishing, because heavy concentrations of insects hatch out on, or fall onto, the water surface and are eaten by trout. It is also the most visually exciting method of fly fishing. A take on the surface means that you'll see not only a swirl or a ring on the water, but probably also the fish itself.

The best practice is to select an artificial fly that matches, as closely as possible, the size, color, and shape of the natural insects you see, or expect to see, on the water. All dry flies should be anointed with some type of floatant—paste, liquid, or spray—so that they will float as high and as long as possible. And before you start fishing in earnest, check that particular fly's stance on the water. Cast it a short way upcurrent and look it over carefully as it floats down past you. An occasional fly that looked great in your box will fail to sit well on

Presenting a dry fly upstream.

the water. Some flop over, unappetizingly, on their sides. Worse still, a few may insist on floating on a vertical, rather than a horizontal, plane with tail and body submerged. Now—before you've wasted a half hour casting it—is the time to discard that rogue fly and tie on another.

The conventional method of presenting a dry fly calls for a cast in an upstream or up-and-across-stream direction, landing the fly about 2 feet directly upcurrent from where you saw either a fish or its riseform. This should allow the imitation to float back downstream like a natural insect. If it skitters or drags across the current unlike the real flies on the water, trout will usually let it pass by, untouched. However, there are a few, but only a few, occasions where it pays to break this rule.

There are some choice places that simply can't be covered from a downstream position. Lies just upstream of major snags or large trees

Capture a live insect, then try to match it from your fly box.

that have been toppled out into the stream flow can only be reached from upcurrent. Stand nearly directly upstream from the fish and let the fly coast down to it on a slack line. Of course, you run the risk of alarming the trout when you pull the fly back at the last moment so that it won't get caught in the branches. However, this trick works often enough to be a valuable tactic, and some of the best fish in any stream occupy these hard-to-reach places.

On other occasions, you may have floated your fly several times over a fish that continues to rise, but ignores your artificial. This usually calls for a change to a better imitation, yet even this doesn't always bring the desired result. As a last resort, give your fly a tiny twitch—only enough to make it twinkle on the surface—just before it passes over the fish. This often convinces a trout that, even though your fly looks a bit different from the ones it's dining on, it is, at least, alive and good to eat, too.

DRY FLY ON STILL WATER

There's little reward in fishing a dry fly on lakes and ponds unless you see fish actively surface-feeding. There's just too much blank territory to prospect with an almost stationary fly. But when fish are rising— and this is quite common on calm evenings—it's the most enjoyable way to catch trout, bass, or panfish.

The traditional method is to cast your fly as close to a riseform as possible and let it sit for 10 or 20 seconds. If it goes untouched, make it jiggle on the water surface, then pause again after this small advertisement. You can usually repeat this procedure several times before the fly becomes drowned. At that point, pick it up and dry it out with a few false casts; then send it out to another likely spot for a repeat performance.

BASS BUGS AND POPPERS

Although these lures are fished on the surface, I can't really call them dry flies—even those that are tied up out of deer hair and then clipped to shape. In fact, only a few of the smaller "bass bugs" imitate any kind of bug. Most of them are supposed to look and act like frogs or injured minnows dying on the surface.

You do present bugs much as you would dry flies, though. You cast them out, let them sit for half a minute, jiggle them a bit, and wait again. You follow the same procedure with a cup-faced popper, only you give this a sharp tug each time to create extra surface disturbance and the loud "pop" that attracts fish from quite a distance. Frog imitations are fished differently and a bit faster. Catch a medium-sized frog and toss it out 30 feet from shore. It'll teach you far better than I can how to make your retrieve.

When fishing for bass and panfish, slow and seductive does it. Most anglers fish these floaters too rapidly. That agonizingly long pause between twitches or tugs really pays off.

On the other hand, when you expect pike or pickerel, speed things up. For some reason, a frog or minnow imitation that appears frightened and eager to leave the vicinity in a hurry seems to excite the killer instinct in these slim, toothy predators.

WET FLY AND NYMPH ON STREAMS

The nymph is designed to imitate the underwater, or larval, forms of several aquatic insects, mainly mayflies, caddisflies, and stoneflies. Wet flies, especially the soft-hackled, no-wing models, are probably mistaken for nymphs, too, though some of the gaudier, winged patterns may suggest tiny fish or fry.

Both of these small, underwater flies are usually fished in essentially the same manner. The standard, and easiest, method is to cast them across and slightly downstream and let them swing with the current through a wide arc on a tight line until they hang in the current straight below you. If you take a step or two downstream after each cast and repeat this process, you can cover virtually all the likely water in a run or pool on a fair-sized stream in a surprisingly short time. This classic, "chuck-and-chance-it" approach may call for minimum finesse, but it is enormously productive—perhaps because the fly passes over so many fish.

There are, of course, infinite variations on this basic theme. The best wet-fly fisherman I know casts his fly slightly upstream, letting it sink and drift for 15 or 20 feet freely with the current; then, as the line tightens, he starts twitching the sunken fly with short pulls on the line until it hangs dead in the water below him. He feels that the free-drifting-and-sinking, first part of this presentation imitates a nymph that has lost its footing and is being swept downstream. The second, or dragging, part of this delivery attempts to convince the trout that the fly, now rising and swinging up overhead, is a nymph swimming toward the surface to hatch out into an air-breathing, adult insect.

An even more sophisticated way to fish these flies is in an upstream manner, drag-free, the way you would fish a dry fly. This is probably the most advanced, difficult form of fly fishing. It is also the most productive. An expert in this discipline can catch trout when all other fly fishers are drawing blanks.

An upstream nymph can fish quite deeply, especially if slightly weighted, because the longer it drifts on a slack line, the farther down it sinks. A trout—even one with little desire to feed—will open its mouth and take a nymph that threatens to bang it on the nose. When water and weather conditions are utterly abominable, this is often the only method (short of live-bait fishing) to catch a few fish.

You can't cover much water fishing this way, so you'll also have to be an expect at reading currents. Concentrate on the known choicest lies where you can pinpoint fish. Learning how quickly or slowly to recover line during each drift, to stay in touch with your fly, takes a lot of judgment and experience. So does detecting the slight pause in the downstream travel of your line, indicating that a fish might have taken your nymph. Such fishing demands the skill and concentration of a brain surgeon, and very few anglers have the patience to master it.

WET FLY AND NYMPH ON LAKES

This is the bread-and-butter method of catching trout in lakes and ponds and, fortunately, not a very demanding one. You cast your fly out over likely territory, or where you've caught fish before, and retrieve it with fairly slow twitches of several inches at a time. Outside of discovering where the trout are on that day, there are only two variations in this rather methodical technique that are left to your discretion.

One decision you have to make is at what depth your fly should travel. Some days (most likely, evenings), fish will take just under the surface, where you can see the swirl of the strike. Other times, you may have to pause for several seconds and let your fly settle a few feet before starting your retrieve. When fishing is especially dour, you may have to resort to a leaded fly and a sinking line to fish near the bottom for a few, apathetic fish that weren't eager enough to swim up a few feet for a free meal. Generally speaking, if fish are feeding well, they'll take near the surface.

The speed of your retrieve is the other variable you'll have to consider. Sometimes tantalizingly slow is best, while on other occasions fish will prefer a fly that's stripped in quite briskly. You never know in advance. Experiment.

The only other lake fish with a fondness for sunken, insect-imitating flies are small bass and most panfish. The methods described above work well for them, too.

STREAMER FLY ON RUNNING WATER

Not only do trout love minnows, but the bigger the fish, the higher the proportion of its smaller relatives that make up its diet. That's why so many of those huge trout that stare down at you, glassy eyed, from the wall were caught on bucktails or streamers. These flies imitate minnows, and they're the trophy fisher's (and the taxidermist's) best friend.

Streamers are usually fished in much the same way as wet flies, only with a bit more vigor. They are cast across and downcurrent at about a 45-degree angle to the flow and twitched or pumped in the current to act like a bait minnow in distress. There's something about an injured or dying minnow that brings out the bully in both trout and bass.

There are two major points to keep in mind when fishing streamers. The first is that they're most effective in fast water—deep runs or heads of pools on modest flows. They're also strong medicine during the torrents of spring or when water levels are up after a summer rain. They're deadliest when they force the fish into making a snap decision.

The other thing to remember about streamers and bucktails is that a poorly timed cast can render them useless. The feathers or hair that make up their "wings" are typically twice as long as the hook shank, and if these get snagged in the bend of the hook, fish won't touch the now off-kilter imitation. (You might think this would make

A self-snapped (and useless) streamer fly.

the fly look and act even more like a crippled minnow, but somehow it doesn't.) On windy or gusty days, I always check my streamer after every few casts, and it can't hurt to take a look every few minutes even on calm days. You can feel pretty stupid when you discover you've been casting for a half hour with a fly that was completely out of commission.

STREAMER ON STILL WATER

Bucktails and streamers are probably the most productive flies for lake-dwelling trout, bass, and pike. Two-inch flies are the usual choice for trout, 3- to 4-inchers for bass; and for pike, go for the biggest and brightest you can buy.

Again, fish them much as you would a wet fly on these waters, only a bit faster and with more pronounced twitches. Sometimes bass, which are inordinately fond of crawfish, will respond to a brownish fly, like the Muddler Minnow, fished slowly and just off the bottom on a sinking line. Pike, on the other hand, show a decided preference for a fast-moving fly.

SALTWATER STREAMER

Since most saltwater gamefish live on baitfish, streamers and buck-tails are the mainstays of the seagoing fly rodder. Big, pike-sized flies are almost always best, but they won't last long in the briny unless they're tied on stainless-steel hooks.

Most saltwater baitfish travel a lot faster than freshwater ones, so your retrieve should usually be brisk. This may mean that you'll have to cast out more often, but it will also mean more strikes.

In a few cases, you'll be hard pressed to move your fly rapidly enough. If fish keep following your fly, then turning away, try a more frenzied retrieve. Some barracuda specialists cast out, jam their rod handle between their legs, and retrieve line hand over hand (yes, with both hands) like madmen. This takes some practice, but the barracudas eat it up.

FLY FISHING THE FLATS

The flats are a world of their own. The fish that feed in this thin water and their food are different from most oceanic types. The bonefish, permit, and redfish that cruise the shallows aren't looking for minnows, but for shrimp and crabs. This sort of food is not swift, but it manages to survive by concealment in the grass or by burrowing in the sand or mud when threatened.

Here, your fly should imitate not only the appearance of crabs or shrimp, but also their scuttling, secretive behavior. Such flies should be tied upside down—that is, with most of the hair or feathers on the underside, instead of on top, of the hook shank—so that the fly will ride hook-point up. A conventionally tied fly will hang up on the bottom or pick up weeds too frequently to be useful here. It's best to cast your fly 10 to 15 feet ahead of a cruising fish, which will minimize your chances of alarming it in such shallow water. Give your fly a couple of good tugs to catch the fish's attention and to make it appear that it is trying to escape. Then let your fly drop quickly to the bottom.

The fish, at this point, should swing over to investigate, but even if it doesn't, you have one last resort. Give your fly another sharp tug, which should kick up sand or a puff of mud from the bottom. That should do it. Now, as the fish approaches, resist the temptation to overdo it and strip the fly again. The fish knows where the fly is, all right. Your job now is to make your imitation act as if it were trying to burrow out of sight.

Try to just jiggle the fly on the bottom. If the fish starts to turn away, twitch a little harder, but don't strip. Stay with your game plan. The fish may, indeed, refuse your fly. Flats fish—especially permit, but also heavily pounded bonefish—can be very picky. But scooting your fly rapidly along the bottom is, at this point, only going to look unrealistic and may, perhaps, alarm the fish. Most anglers manipulate their flats flies far too much.

If the fish is a stationary tailer, your tactics should be slightly different. Cast as close to it as you dare or within, say, a foot or two, and in front of the fish. Let it sink and then twitch it ever so slightly, so that it acts like an animal that's been dislodged by the fish's rooting and is trying to dig down and hide again.

I can't promise you that you'll take every fish you cast to by following these instructions. You'll spook a lot no matter how careful you are. And some days the fish won't take anything. But you'll take your share of them, and a far higher percentage of fish you cast to, than the compulsive stripper will.

Special Situations—Bass

SINCE BLACK bass are the most widely pursued gamefish in North American waters, perhaps they should receive special attention.

There are two species of this largest member of the sunfish family: the largemouth and the smallmouth. (True, taxonomists tell us there are a few other species, but all are of very limited distribution and are fished for in much the same manner as the principal two.)

Fortunately for freshwater anglers, both species are hardy and prolific reproducers. Unlike trout and landlocked salmon, populations are highly self-sustaining and there's almost never a need for restocking once a population has been established.

The largemouth grows to about twice the size of the smallmouth and prefers warmer water. This is the dominant species in the southern portions of the country, while smallmouth are far more numerous in the northern states and on up into Canada.

Largemouths often frequent shallow water and like the shade of weedbeds, lily pads, stumps, and docks. They exhibit no distaste for muddy or roily water and often hang out in sluggish, silt-laden rivers as well as in murky lakes and ponds. They feed primarily on small fish, but will take frogs, if available, and, in fact, anything that moves and will fit into their mouths.

Smallmouths are more finicky. They have a decided appetite for crawfish, although they, too, will take minnows and frogs. They prefer rocky shorelines, lake bottoms, or riverbeds where crawfish are most abundant, and show a strong preference for clear water. When surface water temperatures rise in summer, they seek the coolness of deeper water, often 20 to 30 feet down and only venture into the food-rich shallows at dusk, dawn, or nighttime—when the water cools down a bit.

Until after the turn of the century, fly fishing for both species was done mainly with oversized wet flies—mostly blown-up patterns of the gaudy, brook trout flies of the day—and often attached behind a small spinner. But when the streamer fly emerged from Maine it soon displaced the chunkier wets, and, at about the same time, surface lures of cork or clipped deer hair became popular.

Most bass fly fishers prefer 7- or 8-weight fly rods with a slow action that allows the wind-resistant lures time to turn over and straighten out the leader. A few specialists go to 10- or 11-weight so they can cast the very largest flies, which often attract the largest largemouth bass. Double-tapered lines as well as weight-forward can be used because heroic distance is seldom called for. A salmon-strength leader—8- to 12-pound test—can be used because bass are seldom gut-shy and a strong leader helps to roll over the bulky fly or bug; it also comes in handy when you want to turn fish away from snags or haul them out of weedbeds.

Almost any decent fly reel will do. A heavy drag is not necessary, and there's little need for backing since bass almost never make long runs.

Surface lures of deer hair, cork, or plastic perhaps are most effective on the shallow-dwelling largemouths, although they'll hit streamers well, too. Smallmouths like poppers, too, but when they're in deeper water are usually best fished for with a well-weighted streamer on a sink-tip line. Muddlers, Clouser Minnows, and the many crawfish imitations are all popular choices.

While there are some days—or times of day—when bass will hit your streamer at any speed of travel, a moderate retrieve in series of short strips usually is most effective. When you're after largemouths, a slighter slower strip is best.

Surface lures—whether they imitate frogs, injured minnows, or God-knows-what—are best fished slowly, even teasingly. The general rule is to wait until the ripples made by your bug hitting the water die down before giving it a twitch or a gurgle. Then wait a similar period before repeating the process. Using flies with a simple weed-guard will enable you to fish them in and around weedbeds and even over fallen trees.

When hooked, bass are usually best played out with a firm hand. When they run, let them take line; but remember that your heavy leader will allow you to put great pressure on a fish. When you stop them, put on pressure and try to regain line.

Both fish are acrobatic leapers. When they erupt out of the water, lower your rod and bow to them the way you would to a tarpon or a salmon.

The smallmouth is the gamier of the two fish. Pound for pound, it is a stronger and decidedly quicker fish. Since largemouths are of larger than average size, many fly fishers prefer them.

Both are extremely obliging when it comes time to boat them. There's no need for a net and certainly none for a gaff. When they're on their sides and obviously played out, just reach down and grab them by the lower jaw. Their teeth are rough, but not sharp. Then bend the jaw down and raise them out of the water. This seems to paralyze them, and they'll stay docile while you remove the hook. It's as simple as that.

Both bass are wonderful gamefish for the fly rod. Nothing in freshwater fishing quite compares to the huge rise of a largemouth bass to a bug at dusk. Someone compared the splash to that made when a fire bucket is thrown into the calm surface.

CHAPTER

Special Situations— Salt Water

BY FAR the fastest growing type of angling is saltwater fly fishing. Every year, the ranks of briny fly casters seem to double and the end is not yet in sight.

Then, too, every year new species seem to be targeted. I recently read of a small group of Northwestern anglers who were regularly catching cod and halibut with fast-sinking lines. Part of this growth is due to the fact that this sport is relatively new. Before World War II, standard fly fishing gear consisted of varnished, split-cane rods, silk lines, and silkworm gut leaders. All of these were highly perishable when exposed to the corrosive power of salt water—even when washed down carefully after each use. The salmon reels of the time couldn't handle the rigors of salt water, either.

The fairly recent—and nearly simultaneous—invention of nylon monofilament, fiberglass (and, slightly later, graphite), and plastic-coated fly lines changed all that. Most large fly reels are now salt-water tolerant, too.

That's not to say that saltwater fly fishing is a totally new sport. The famous bassologist Dr. James Henshall wrote about his successful fly fishing in southern Florida with a few friends back in the 1880s. He's vague about species taken. Probably sea trout, snook, and red-fish. If he'd tied into tarpon or bonefish, he'd probably have been impressed enough to mention it. Presumably, he was using freshwater salmon tackle.

In New England, Stan Gibbs experimented with fly patterns for striped bass in the '20s and '30s. One of his flies, the Gibbs Striper, survives to this day. However, he enlisted few recruits, probably due to the same tackle limitations.

Most saltwater gamefish not only average larger than freshwater fish, but are harder fighters for their size. If tied together, a 10-pound bonefish on its initial run would tear the tail off a 10-pound Atlantic salmon. And a baby tarpon will jump far higher and more often than any bass of the same size.

This is the reason why saltwater fly tackle is considerably stouter than that used in fresh water. Rods of 8- or 9-weight are for openers. These are standard for sea trout, snook, bonefish, and redfish in the South and for stripers, blues, and false albacore in the North.

Most rods are 9 feet, though I have a fondness for 9½-footers. Reels have 3¾-inch spools and carry at least 200 yards of 20 pound-test backing. Tippets are usually 10- to 12-pound-test and up.

For giant tarpon, you have to step up a bit: 11- and 12-weight rods come into play here and reels should hold up to 300 yards of 30-pound-test under the fly line.

If you venture out into blue water for billfish, even tarpon tackle won't do the job. A 13-weight rod or better is called for here, and you'll need even more and stronger backing no matter how quickly the captain follows the fish.

A further reason for this up-sizing of rods and lines for salt water is that you're not only casting larger flies, but you're usually fighting stronger winds as well, never mind the fish. Fifteen knots over open ocean water is rated benign, and it goes on up from there.

There are so many types of fish to cast to in the Atlantic, Pacific, and the Gulf of Mexico that it would become tedious to enumerate all the sizes and patterns of flies used. They would vary from white, tinsel-bodied 2-inch steamers used for snapper blues and tinker mackerel in bays and harbors up to 8-inch or better monsters for pelagic billfish. While most bonefish and permit flies are tied to imitate crabs and shrimp, the vast majority of patterns used for other species imitate some sort of baitfish or, sometimes, squid. Probably the most widely used of all saltwater flies is the Lefty's Deceiver, developed by Lefty Kreh and available in a dozen variations. It's even shown on a U.S. postage stamp.

It is equally difficult to describe the best retrieve or fly manipulation method for so many species. Retrieves will vary from the nearly motionless presentation of a crab fly to a permit up to the frenetic hand-over-hand (with rod handle tucked under your armpit) hauling of a needlefish imitation past the nose of a barracuda. The majority of fish, though, respond to the medium-speed twitch retrieve, much as you'd use in fresh water.

The playing of the fish once hooked, again, varies with the species. When they decide to run, let them have their head, but be sure your drag is set tight enough for that size and species. When they jump, lower the rod quickly so they won't land on a tight leader. And, when they get in relatively close, punish them as much as possible with side pressure. If they run or circle to the left, tilt your rod to the right and exert all the pressure you dare. This tends to break their spirit. Of course this doesn't have much effect if they're out over a hundred feet or more. It's a close-in, finishing-off tactic for large, strong fish.

Similarly, boating your fish depends a lot on size and species. Billfish are usually grabbed by the spike with a gloved hand. Since this can be dangerous, a novice shouldn't attempt it.

Tarpon are sometimes lip gaffed and brought aboard for pictures. However, many guides feel that lifting a heavy fish out of the supporting water may damage internal organs, and they hold the exhausted fish against the side of the boat while the hook is removed.

Some medium-sized fish are probably best netted. Very few fish need to be hauled in with a kill gaff.

The main point is: Treat your catch as gently as you can. Revive it if necessary and release it unless you're certain you want to eat it. It pays to leave some for the next guy—and for the next time you're out.

Many freshwater fly fishers are turning to salt water every year and the reasons are clear: The fish are bigger and more powerful, there's generally less pressure on them, and the variety is inexhaustible. Likewise, many bait-and-plug saltwater anglers are turning to the fly rod because it is challenging, rewarding, and lots of fun.

9

Hooking, Playing, and Landing

"... my bended hook shall pierce
Their slimy jaws ..."
—William Shakespeare,
Antony and Cleopatra

CONGRATULATIONS! You've done everything right so far, and you've inveigled a fish into taking your fly. Now what?

SETTING THE HOOK

Artificial flies don't taste like natural food and most don't even have a similar texture, so they're usually ejected by the fish shortly after they've been taken. However, some species of fish will mouth a fly longer, or take it in a different manner from others, so the art of hooking fish is one with several subtle variations.

Running Water

Let's take the easiest case first. When you're fishing any type of underwater fly—nymph, wet fly, or streamer—across and downstream in flowing water, your line is tight and you should strike the instant you

feel a fish touch your fly. By this, I don't mean you should try to yank its head off. More than 90 percent of all trout broken off are lost through heavy-handed striking. A quick, but gentle, twitch of the wrist is enough to ensure that the hook is pulled in over the barb. In fact, the fish will often hook itself before you have time to react, and nothing could be simpler than that.

However, when anglers fish wets and streamers in this standard manner, too many fish are missed. You feel a thump and they're gone before you have time to strike. This, unfortunately, is one of the drawbacks of this technique, but there is something you can do to hook a higher percentage of fish. Try to cast an absolutely straight line onto the water and to keep it straight, without bellying, during the swing. It's surprising how many more fish you'll hook firmly when you're in direct contact with your fly at all times.

Striking a fish that takes a dry fly is quite different. Here, you should hook a much higher percentage of takers because, since you're casting upstream, you're pulling the fly back into the fish's mouth. (In downstream fishing, you're actually yanking the fly away from the fish.) And since the fish isn't instantaneously pricked by the hook, you can afford a slight pause before striking.

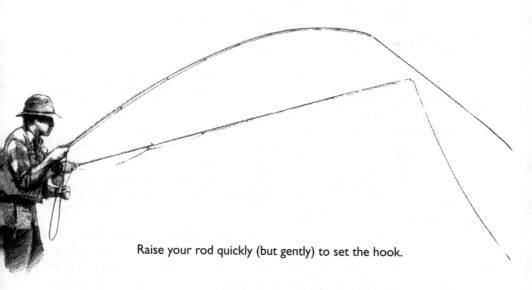

Raise your rod quickly (but gently) to set the hook.

Probably a fish that has risen up to the surface—a zone of jeopardy—wants to get back down to its lie before sorting out what it has managed to grab. Whatever the reason, trout will hold a dry fly in their mouths for as much as several seconds before spitting it out. British chalk-stream anglers maintain that, when a trout takes a floater, you should wait until after you've intoned "God save the queen" before striking.

I'll have to confess that at such moments I'm seldom preoccupied with the salvation of the queen, but I do wait about a second before making contact. If you think of this act as more of a quick tightening than a true strike, you'll save a lot of flies and tippet material. The majority of anglers hit a rising fish both too quickly and too heftily.

You should be even more deliberate and tentative when fishing tiny flies (size 18 or smaller) or the spent-wing imitations of dead mayflies at dusk. Both types of artificials are virtually impossible to see on the water, so it's a mistake to rear back when you see a dimple or ring appear in the vicinity of your fly. If the trout has taken a nearby natural instead, ripping your fly across the water may put the fish down. If, on the other hand, the fish has taken, a hearty strike will all too often snap the leader. And if this happens in late evening, it's usually too dark to tie on another one. The best procedure here is to wait a second, raise your rod slowly, and feel for contact with the fish. Slight rod tension is usually enough to set these small hooks securely.

Still Waters

Wet- and streamer-fly fishing on lakes calls for a different hook-setting technique. Twitch-retrieve with your left hand pulling the line. Don't try to add action by twitching the rod tip. Your rod should stay motionless, pointing directly down the path of the line. After each draw, pinch the line under the forefinger of your right, or rod, hand (see illustration) so that it's always under tension. When you do feel a fish tighten, do *not* raise your rod tip for a conventional strike. Just keep retrieving at the same pace until the rod bucks and the fish takes off. Then raise your rod.

Why this is more effective than striking as you would in running water, I don't know. I have never been submerged with mask and snorkel nearby when a fish took a streamer in still water. But any Maine guide will promise you that this is the surest way to hook

Hand and line positions for wet-fly or streamer retrieve.

trout, bass, or landlocked salmon on wets and streamers, and he's absolutely right.

Bass bugs and poppers, on the other hand, call for instant retaliation. The moment you see the swirl or splash of the fish, strike—and this time I really mean it. Most bugs are tied on big, heavy-wire hooks, and it takes a healthy yank to pull this over the barb into a bass's tough mouth. A flabby strike will usually mean that your popper will be tossed free on the first, head-shaking jump.

While retrieving or manipulating your bug, point your rod straight down the line, exactly as you would when retrieving a streamer. Only this time, you should make the strike by both hauling back on the line with your left hand and raising your rod sharply. You can afford this strong, two-fisted strike because a bug leader is usually plenty strong.

It's almost impossible to strike too quickly, and it's easy to strike too late. Only on those rare occasions when you see the fish swimming up under your bug could you snatch it away prematurely. Under usual sighting conditions, though, and with the relatively long line you're casting, the fish will have your bug firmly in its mouth and will already be headed for the bottom by the time your strike energy reaches him.

Salt Water

Fishing streamers in salt water calls for much the same tactics you'd use on lakes, except everything is a bit more heroic and vigorous. You should be using a relatively strong leader in this game, so there should be no worry about breakage. Once you feel the fish has fastened, rear back hard. Big, stainless-steel hooks don't penetrate easily, so hitting a fish hard and even doing it twice is good insurance.

Flats

Again, fish on the saltwater flats behave differently than other saltwater species. Usually, the only sign that a fish is taking your fly is a tilting of its head toward the bottom. You seldom feel the strike. But if the surface isn't too ruffled, you can see the fish nose down quite clearly. Wait a second or even two, then draw in a foot or so of line slowly and feel for the fish. If it's still only looking, all is not lost (as would be so with a full-fledged strike). With this tentative move, your fly will only scoot along the bottom for a foot or so, and you're still in the ballgame.

If, however, you feel solid contact, strike hard and with both hands at the same time. Quickly do it again. Hit three times if you can. Bonefish have leathery mouths. But hit them only during that short truce bonefish usually agree to before they realize they're in trouble. Once they start their dash, don't try to set the hook again. That would be risking a break-off—even with a stout 10- or 12-pound-test tippet.

PLAYING A FISH

When it comes to playing and landing fish, the fly rod really shines. Being the most delicate and sensitive of rods, it magnifies the fight and transmits every throb and move of the fish intimately to the hand of the angler. A 2-pound fish is more fun on the long rod than a 4-pounder is on bait-casting or spinning tackle.

The fly rod is also the deadliest instrument. A long, supple rod cushions the shocks so that even a lightly hooked fish can usually be landed. And its greater leverage helps you guide the fish in the direction you want.

When stream or river fishing, try to conduct the fight from a position directly crosscurrent from the fish. This will tire it faster and tend to keep the hook firmly lodged. Keep your rod tip high and well bent at all times. If a sizable fish makes a determined run, relax pressure and let the fish go, pulling line off the reel. The minute the fish stops or turns, put the pressure back on again. Don't try to pull a fish back upcurrent, but follow rapidly until you're abreast of it again. Then keep it working.

Always play a fish relatively hard. You'll be doing yourself and the fish a favor. By "hard" I don't mean ham-fisted horsing. But tire the fish out quickly (then either kill or release it) by applying steady pressure up near the limit of what your tippet and hook size can withstand. The longer you play a fish, the greater the chance of losing it and the poorer the odds of the fish recovering from the fight if released.

If a large fish tries to sulk in slack water, get it moving again as soon as possible. Get below it and try to pull it off balance. Pluck the tight line to annoy it. Don't give it a breather or it'll get a second wind and prolong the fight.

Try to keep the fish working in a fairly strong current. Here it'll have to fight both the rod and the flow. When it's in close, hold your rod to the side, parallel to the water, but keep the same bend in it. It's this side pressure that makes swimming difficult and tiring. Pulling upward on a fish won't fatigue it nearly as much.

On ponds and lakes or in the ocean, currents can't help you tire a fish, but your general tactics should be the same. Try to maintain steady, even pressure at all times except during determined runs. Keep the fish on the move without any rest periods.

You can usually tell when a fish is playing out. First, its runs will get shorter and shorter until they're reduced to small surges. Then the fish will start rolling over on its side, an obvious sign of fatigue. Very soon now, you should be able to land it.

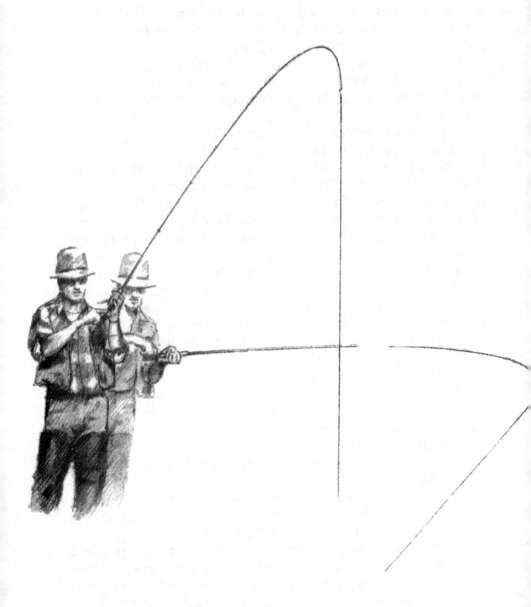

Hold the rod tip high when playing a fish, but lower it to horizontal when the fish is near you.

Landing

Most fish are finally captured in a landing net, but if you forget to bring one or it's out of reach, you can beach fish—even quite large ones—if the terrain is suitable. Gaffing and tailing are now such rare, and often outlawed, methods that I won't describe them here.

Never try to land a fish by sweeping the net toward it. Make the fish swim into it, headfirst, while you hold it stationary. Submerge the rim just under the surface, tilted at a 30- to 45-degree angle, get the fish's head up on the surface, and slowly lead or pull it over the net. Only when most or all of its body is over the bag should you lift the net.

In running water, it's best to face upcurrent, so the bag will extend downstream. This may mean that you'll have to step slightly downcurrent from the fish for this final maneuver and bring it down

A tired trout being netted properly.

to the net. Again, the fish's head should be on, or slightly above, the surface. Fish also seem more docile, or less likely to see the net, if they're lying flat on their sides, too.

Bass, and perhaps a few larger panfish, can be landed by an easy method involving no extra equipment. As a played-out fish comes within reach, put your thumb in its mouth, bend the lower jaw down, and pull the fish out of the water. This lower-jaw grip seems to paralyze, or at least tranquilize, bass. Never attempt this with toothy species such as pike and barracudas, for obvious reasons.

Beaching is a tricky, last-resort business that is only possible on accommodating terrain. You'll need a gently sloping beach or cobble shallows and at least 20 feet of room behind you. When the fish is on its side in the shallows, point the rod toward the fish with only a slight bend in it and start backing up.

If the fish panics and heads for deeper water, as it often will, let it go. Then bring it slowly back to the original position, its head directly

A captured—and pacified—bass.

toward you, and start backing steadily up the beach. Once the fish's body hits the sand or gravel, it will usually start flopping. Now, if you keep applying firm, steady pressure by backing up more rapidly, the fish will keep "swimming" on dry land until it's a safe distance above the waterline. Admittedly, this game takes a little practice, but it comes in handy and sometimes it's the only game in town.

CHAPTER 10

How to Become Expert

"Practice ... practice ... practice!"
—Paul Hornung

A S I STATED in an early chapter, I don't believe a beginner can learn fly casting or fly fishing from a standing start by reading any book. There are just too many subtle points that can only be learned from demonstration and observation. Yet I am equally convinced that reading is one of the surest ways to improve your performance once you've mastered the basics. Again, let me recommend the book listed in appendix 7. Videocassettes can help, too, but they don't offer anything like the wealth of information you'll find in a good angling library.

There are several excellent magazines that can keep you posted on new fly patterns and innovative presentations. Some of these flies and techniques may not prove helpful on the waters you fish, but somebody has worked hard to develop them and believes they're superior, so they're worth a try.

You may also profit from joining a local chapter of Trout Unlimited, Federation of Fly Fishers, or some other angling club (see appendix 7). You can learn a lot from listening to fellow members—not the least of which may be new and better places to fish.

By all means practice casting as often as you can, at least until you're an intermediate fly fisher or better. Only when you can cast proficiently and automatically can you concentrate fully on the fish and on your presentation.

Field study can pay big dividends, too. Learn all you can about water and currents. Study depth charts of nearby lakes and coastlines.

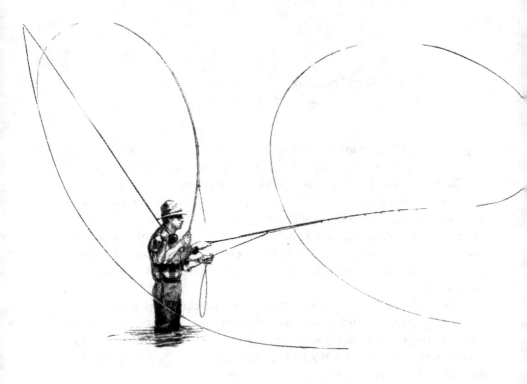

Collect and examine the insects, minnows, and crustaceans your fish feed on and observe their behavior.

By all means keep a fishing diary. After each trip, jot down weather and water conditions, area fished, fish seen, fish caught, flies used, failures, and successes. What natural insects did you see? How did they behave? How did fish rise to them? Reread your notes from time to time. It's surprising how much you can learn from your own experiences.

It is extremely important to acquire the best flies possible. Not the most, just the very best. I know anglers who have spent many thousands of dollars for big collections of expensive rods and reels, yet their fly boxes are filled with junk. I can't comprehend this. Fish can't be impressed by rods and reels. The only part of your tackle they're ever supposed to see, after all, is the fly at the very end of it all.

I wish I could tell you how to distinguish a superb fly from a poor one, but there are just too many types of flies. Words might not be too helpful, anyway, because some qualities defy description. Therefore, my best advice is to find out who ties, or carries, the best flies in your area and then get an expert friend to help you make a selection.

There are no written rules on behavior or etiquette for fly fishers, but there is a general consensus on some Dos and Don'ts. Most of these spring from a simple respect for the environment or for your fellow angler and are so close to good manners in general that I almost hesitate to mention them.

Don't leave litter and don't trespass on private property unless you've first asked for permission. Every year, more and more private land is posted against public access, and the above two offenses are usually given as the reasons.

Since fish are a finite resource—yes, even in salt water—kill only fish you want to eat. Snook and redfish populations have recently become alarmingly low. Tarpon, sailfish, and bonefish are poor eating and should not be killed just to satisfy a "show-and-tell" vanity. Release all undersized or unwanted fish with tender loving care so that they may live to be caught again.

Keep a respectful distance between yourself and other anglers. This is as true for boat fishermen as it is for those afoot. There are, unfortunately, no laws or penalties against roaring up to a school of surface-feeding fish, cutting the throttle at the last instant, and driving

the fish down and away from other fishermen who were there first, but it's obviously slob behavior.

Similarly, when fishing a stream, especially smallish ones, give the angler there ahead of you the courtesy of his obvious priority. Don't crowd in close to him. If he's fishing downstream, start a decent distance upstream of him. Grant him the same deference and space if he's fishing upstream by starting in well downstream.

Last, you don't have to be an expert to get great enjoyment out of fly fishing. But I think you'll agree that the better your performance in any sport, the more pleasure you get from it. So I would now like to think that, since you've read this far, you're already a bit more proficient at fly fishing and that you will find it even more rewarding.

Hook Size Chart

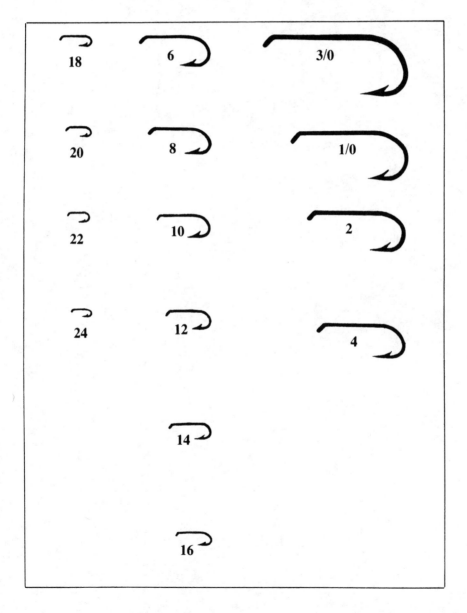

Some Basic, Recommended Flies and Sizes

Dry Flies

Quill Gordon #12, #14
March Brown #10, #12
Light Cahill #12, #14, #16
Adams #12, #14, #16
Hair-Wing Royal Coachman #12, #14, #16
Gray Fox Variant #12, #14, #16
Dun Variant #12, #14
Blue Caddis #14, #16
Tan Caddis #14, #16, #18
Henryville #14, #16, #18
Black Ant #12, #14

Nymphs

Cream #12, #14, #16
Tan #12, #14, #16
Black #12, #14, #16
Hare's Ear #10, #12, #14
Pheasant Tail #12, #14, #16
Yellow Stonefly #8, #10
Black Stonefly #6, #8
Montana #8, #10
Breadcrust #12, #14
Blue Caddis Emerger #12, #14
Brown Caddis Emerger #12, #14

Bass Bugs

(Small, Medium, and Large)
Deer Hair Frog
Injured Minnow
Popper
Dragonfly Bug

Wet Flies

Gold-Ribbed Hare's Ear #12, #14
Leadwing Coachman #10, #12
Royal Coachman #10, #12, #14
March Brown #10, #12
Light Cahill #12, #14, #16
Black Gnat #12, #14
Blue Dun #12, #14, #16

Streamers

(Sizes 2–10, long shank)
Muddler Minnow
Mickey Finn
Gray Ghost
Black-Nosed Dace
Nine-Three
San Juan Worm
Black Marabou
Yellow Marabou

White Marabou
Black Ghost

SALT WATER

White Deceiver #2/0, #2
Blue/White Deceiver #2/0, #2
Yellow Deceiver #2/0, #2
Tarpon Special #3/0
White Skipping Bug #2/0

FLATS

(Sizes 2–6)
Pink Shrimp
Honey Blonde
Crazy Ike (White)
Crazy Ike (Tan)
Crazy Charlie (Pink)

Recommended Leader Tippet Strength by Fly Size

FLY-HOOK SIZE	DIAMETER (IN THOUSANDTHS OF AN INCH)	POUND TEST
20, 22, 24	.004	2
16, 18, 20	.005	3
12, 14, 16	.006	4
10, 12, 14	.007	5
8, 10, 12	.008	6
4, 6, 8	.009	7
1/0, 2, 4	.010	8.5
1/0–5/0	.011+	10–15

Fly Fisherman's Checklist

NECESSITIES

Rod
Reel (with line)
Leader
Fly boxes
Tippet material
Floatant
Boots (or waders)
Hat
Polarized sunglasses
Nail clipper or scissors
License

USEFUL EXTRAS

Stream thermometer
Vest
Rain jacket
Spare reel (with line)
Extra leaders
Line dressing
Leader straightener
Leader sink
Hook hone
Hemostat
Wading staff
Stiletto (for picking out knots)
Small flashlight

OPTIONAL

Wader repair kit
Rod repair kit
Aquarium net
Specimen bottles
Knot-tying tool
Long-nose pliers
First-aid kit
Camera
Insect repellent

Gamefish Temperature and Food Preferences

Fish	Temperature	Food
	Fresh Water	
Trout	Cool, 50s, 60s	Insects, minnows
Bass (smallmouth)	Medium, 60s, 70s	Crawfish, minnows, insects
Bass (largemouth)	Warm, 70s, 80s	Small fish, crawfish, frogs
Pike	Medium, 60s, 70s	Small fish
Pickerel	Medium, 60s, 70s	Small fish
Bluegill	Warm, 70s, 80s	Insects
Yellow perch	Warm, 70s, 80s	Insects, minnows
	Salt Water	
Striped bass	Medium, 60s, 70s	Small fish
Bluefish	Medium, 60s, 70s	Small fish
Mackerel	Medium, 60s, 70s	Small fish
Barracuda	Warm, 70s, 80s	Fish
Snook	Warm, 70s, 80s	Small fish, shrimp
Tarpon	Warm, 70s, 80s	Small fish
	Flats	
Bonefish	Warm, 70s, 80s	Shrimp, crabs
Permit	Warm, 70s, 80s	Crabs, shrimp
Redfish	Warm, 70s, 80s	Shrimp, crabs, minnows

A Glossary of Common Fly Fishing Terms

Aquatic insects. Insects such as mayflies, caddisflies, and stoneflies that spend their early lives under water.

Backcast. That portion of the common overhead cast when the line is propelled to the rear, behind the angler.

Backing line. Strong, thin, usually braided or multifilament line put on the reel before the fly line to fill out the spool and for insurance in case a fish makes a long run.

Belly. The fattest, heaviest portion of a tapered fly line. Also, any pronounced curve in the position of the extended fly line.

Current tongue. The thread, or fastest part, of any current.

Drag. Any influence on fly line or leader that makes a fly travel at a speed different from the current or flow.

Drift food. Any food item, usually an insect or crustacean, that is floating on, or suspended in, the water.

Drown. A dry fly or a floating line is said to "drown" when it gets pulled under the water surface.

Dry fly. A fly, usually quite bushy in appearance, that is tied to exploit surface tension and float on top of the water.

Eddy. Any small or large whirlpool on flowing water.

False cast. Any cast where the line is kept in the air and not allowed to fall on the water.

Fast-action rod. A fly rod that flexes mostly near the tip so that, when bent, it snaps back to a straight position relatively quickly.

Floating line. A fly line with a density lighter than water so that it will float without greasing.

Fly floatant. A water-repellent paste or liquid that helps a dry fly float higher and longer.

Forward cast. The second part of a regular cast, where the line is propelled forward and in front of the angler.

Hatch. As a verb, an aquatic insect's shedding of its nymphal shuck (usually on the water surface) to become a winged adult. As a noun, that period of time (often too brief) when many insects are on the water.

Leader. A length of less visible monofilament (usually tapered) between the heavier fly line and the fly.

Lie. The fairly stationary feeding or holding position of a fish in running water.

Limestone stream. A usually slow-moving, often weedy stream that has a high pH and is rich in fish food.

Line speed. The speed at which the unstraightened part of a fly line (and the fly) is traveling during a cast.

Monofilament. A single-strand, transparent material, usually of nylon, that is used for leaders.

Natural. The real insect or crustacean that fish feed on, as opposed to the angler's imitation.

Open loop. A wide curve in the fly line as it travels forward or backward during casting.

Overhead cast. The most common cast in fly fishing, in which the rod is held in a vertical, or near-vertical, position.

Pocket. A miniature pool in a run or riffle, usually created by an emerging rock or boulder.

Pool. A slow, deep portion of a river or stream where the gradient temporarily levels out.

Presentation. The manner in which a fly lands on the water and how it is made to behave in the fishing area.

Prick. To scratch, or hook only momentarily, a fish that has taken the fly. Such fish will rarely strike a second time.

Power stroke. That brief period during a forward or backward cast when power is applied by the rod hand.

Read. The act of analyzing a stream or river from clues provided by depth, cover, and currents to determine where the fish should lie.

Riffle. A fast portion of running water, usually shallow and containing few good fish.

Rise. The upward motion of a fish toward either a natural or artificial food item—usually, but not always, breaking the surface.

Riseform. The disturbance left on the surface by a rising fish. This is most often a spreading circle.

Roll cast. A maneuver in which the line is rolled out over the water without any backcast.

Rough stream. Also spate, rainfed, or freestone stream. These are usually characterized by rubble and boulder streambeds, rather steep gradients, and frequent flooding. The majority of our streams fall into this category.

Rubble. Stones larger than gravel, but smaller than slabs or boulders.

Run. A fast portion of a stream or river, narrower and deeper than a riffle. These are good trout-holding places, especially in summer.

Running line. The thin portion of any weight-forward fly line behind the belly.

Shoot. To let out extra line during the forward or backward cast to increase the distance of a cast.

Sidearm cast. Precisely the same as the overhead cast except that all motions are carried out in a more horizontal plane.

Sinking line. All fly lines with a specific gravity heavier than water. There is now an astonishing variety—from ultrafast sinkers to slow, medium, and fast sinkers—including various ones where the body of the line floats and only the end portion sinks.

Slow-action rod. A fly rod that bends down into the grip when flexed. Such rods are slower in their snap-back time and aren't so demanding of perfect timing on the part of the caster.

Spring creek. A usually slow-moving stream from sand country—not as rich as a limestoner, but having many of the same qualities.

Still water. A pond or lake. Any body of water where current is not a factor.

Strike. The act of a fish taking a fly. Also the angler's reaction to set the hook when a fish has taken.

Strip. To pull in line, after the cast has been made, with the left or line hand, manipulating the fly in a series of jerks.

Sunken fly. Any fly fished below the surface: wet flies, nymphs, streamers, bucktails.

Tailing. When fish are bottom-feeding in shallow water, their tails often break the surface. Such easily spotted fish are called "tailers."

Tailing loop. When the loop formed by the unrolling fly line has an arc greater than 180 degrees, it has a "closed" or "tailing" loop. This is the greatest cause of casting knots into a leader.

Tight loop. If the loop formed by the unrolling fly line is 2 feet wide or less, it can be considered "tight." If it measures 3 feet or more, it is "open."

Tippet. The last and thinnest strand of a tapered leader—the one to which the fly is tied.

Traveling loop. The loop formed by an unrolling fly line.

References

BOOKS

Art Flick's Master Fly-Tying Guide by Art Flick et al. Crown, 1972, Lyons Press, 1984. Experts share their fly-tying tricks and techniques.

Fly Fishing for Bonefish by Dick Brown. Lyons Press, 1993. A thorough treatise on the subject.

Fly Fishing for Smallmouth Bass by Harry Murray. Lyons Press, 1989. A pathbreaking guide to a growing sport.

Hatches by Al Caucci and Bob Natasi. Comparahatch, Ltd., 1975. Word and color-photo guide to North American mayflies.

Lamar Underwood's Bass Almanac. Lyons Press, 1979. Experts reveal their secrets for taking America's most popular gamefish.

Masters on the Dry Fly ed. by J. Migel. Lippincott, 1977. Top dry-fly men give a detailed "how-to" course.

Masters on the Nymph ed. by J. Migel and L. Wright. Lyons Press, 1979. Mysteries of successful nymph fishing explained by master nymphers.

A Modern Dry-Fly Code by Vincent Marinaro. Lyons Press, 1983. Flies and tactics for fishing limestone and spring creeks.

The Orvis Fly-Fishing Guide by Tom Rosenbauer. Lyons Press, 1984. Complete and clear—ideal for the beginning or intermediate fly fisher.

Selective Trout by Doug Swisher and Carl Richards. Crown, 1971, Lyons Press, 1985. How to outwit smart and choosy trout.

Stillwater Trout ed. by J. Merwin. Lyons Press, 1980. Special techniques and winning flies for ponds and lakes.

Trout by Ray Bergman. Knopf, 1938. After more than 60 years, still some of the best and wisest advice.

MAGAZINES

Field & Stream, 2 Park Avenue, New York, NY 10016

The Flyfisher, P.O. Box 722, Sandpoint, ID 83864

Flyfishing, 4040 S.E. Wister, Portland, OR 97222
Fly Fisherman Magazine, 6405 Flank Drive, Harrisburg, PA 17112
Fly Rod & Reel, P.O. Box 370, Camden, ME 04843
Trout, 1500 Wilson Boulevard, Suite 310, Arlington, VA 22209

RECOMMENDED JOINING

Federation of Fly Fishers, P.O. Box 1595, Bozeman, MT 59771
Trout Unlimited, 1500 Wilson Boulevard, Suite 310, Arlington, VA 22209

Index